D1116331

MEAN MACHINES

SUPERPLANES

PAUL HARRISON

ARCTURUS

Reprinted 2013

This edition first published in 2012 by Arcturus Publishing

Distributed by Black Rabbit Books
P. O. Box 3263
Mankato
Minnesota MN 56002

Copyright © 2012 Arcturus Publishing Limited

Printed in the USA

Library of Congress Cataloging-in-Publication Data

Harrison, Paul, 1969-
 Superplanes / by Paul Harrison.
    p. cm. -- (Mean machines)
 Includes index.
 ISBN 978-1-84858-565-2 (hardcover, library bound)
 1. Airplanes--Juvenile literature. I. Title.
 TL547.H245 2013
 629.133'34--dc23

                            2011051517

Text: Paul Harrison
Editor: Joe Harris
Design: sprout.uk.com
Cover design: sprout.uk.com

Picture credits:
Cover: left ©Mike Fizer/Transtock/Corbis; top right: © US Air Force - digital version c/Science
Faction/Corbis; bottom right © George Hall/CORBIS. Airbus S.A.S. 2005—exm company/S.
Ognier: 15. Airbus S.A.S. 2011-computer rendering Fixion: 14–15. Alain Nogues/Sygma/Corbis:
12t. Antonov Airlines: 13. Bombardier Aerospace: 22. Dornier Seaplane: 18, 19. George Hall/
Corbis: cover (r), 12b. Gulfstream Aerospace Corporation: 16, 17. Image provided courtesy of
Northrop Grumman: 8, 9. Jim Sugar/Corbis: 6t, 7. Keith Wilson/Optica.co.uk: 20–21. Lockheed
Martin Corporation: 3, 10t, 10b, 11. Mark Greenberg/Virgin Galactic: 30, 30–31, 31t, 31b.
Meoita/Shutterstock.com: 25. Mike Fizer/Transtock/Corbis: cover (l), 26–27. NASA: 4 (main), 5.
NASA-digital version/Science Faction/Corbis: 4 (inset) Paul Drabot/Shutterstock.com: 28b. Phil
Emmerson/Shutterstock.com: 28–29. Susan&Allan Parker/Alamy: 24t. Thierry Grun-Aero/Alamy:
24b. Toby Melville/Reuters/Corbis: 6b. US Air Force-digital version c/Science Faction/Corbis:
cover (t), 1. William Attard McCarthy/Shutterstock.com: 23.

SL002136US
Supplier 02, Date 0113, Print Run 2499

CONTENTS

SUPERPLANES

X-43A

Planes are the kings of the sky. No other vehicles (apart from spacecraft) can match them for soaring elegance and blistering speed. This book is about the most amazing aircraft: the superplanes. Perhaps the most "super" of all is the X-43A, the fastest plane on Earth.

The X-43A takes a piggyback on another plane.

When the plane reaches 40,000 ft. (12,000 m), the booster unit is set free.

The X-43A, which is mounted at the front end of the booster unit, is released when it reaches around 90,000 ft. (27,500 m).

The X-43A is made by NASA, the government agency in charge of space exploration. It has no room for passengers—or even a pilot. Each X-43A lasts for just one flight, before it is deliberately crashed. It is an experimental plane and is used to test out new technology and ideas about flight.

The X-43A uses a type of engine called a scramjet. This uses fast-moving air mixed with hydrogen fuel to provide the power.

Its top speed is a remarkable Mach 9.6, which is nearly 7,000 mph (11,200 km/h).

SUPER STATS

X-43A
LENGTH: 12 ft. (3.7 m)
WINGSPAN: 5 ft. (1.5 m)
RANGE: (estimated) 900 miles (1,450 km)
NUMBER OF CREW: 0
NUMBER OF PASSENGERS: 0
TOP SPEED: Mach 9.6

VIRGIN ATLANTIC
GLOBALFLYER

Today it's possible for planes to fly right around the world without landing. The trick is to stay in the air with the least fuel possible. The GlobalFlyer was designed and built with one purpose in mind— to beat the record for the distance covered by a plane without refueling.

At 114 ft. (35 m), GlobalFlyer's wings are as wide as a passenger jet airliner.

Remarkably, GlobalFlyer has just one jet engine.

The wings are made from carbon fiber, which is both very light and very strong.

Breaking the distance record in 2005 meant traveling all the way around the world nonstop. And this is exactly what pilot Steve Fosset managed in 76 hours, 42 minutes, and 55 seconds. In 2006, he flew even farther. The 2006 journey took GlobalFlyer from Florida all the way around the world and then onward to Bournemouth, Great Britain.

The plane needs parachutes to slow it down when coming in to land.

GlobalFlyer has 13 fuel tanks, which together hold 18,700 lbs. (8,480 kg) of fuel.

SUPER STATS

VIRGIN ATLANTIC GLOBALFLYER
LENGTH: 38 ft., 6 in. (11.8 m)
WINGSPAN: 114 ft. (35 m)
RANGE: (estimated) 25,884 miles (41,657 km)
NUMBER OF CREW: 1
NUMBER OF PASSENGERS: 0
TOP SPEED: 342.24 mph (550.8 km/h)

NORTHROP GRUMMAN B-2 SPIRIT

Advances in technology are often driven by the military. The B-2 Spirit is an extraordinary warplane belonging to the United States Air Force. It's often called the "stealth bomber." It's one of the most advanced superplanes in existence.

The shape of the B-2 is called a "flying wing." This means the front edges of wings are angled at 33° and the rear of the wing is in a "w" shape.

The B-2 can fly around 6,000 miles (9,600 km) without being refueled.

Refueling can happen in midair! This gives the B-2 an overall range of around 10,000 miles (16,000 km).

The height a plane travels above sea level is called its altitude. The B-2 can fly at a maximum altitude of 50,000 ft. (15,200 m).

The military is normally able to track planes using radar. However, the B-2 Spirit is incredibly difficult to detect. The shape of the plane, the amount of noise it makes, and even the type of paint used on it make it almost impossible to spot. This is good news for the pilot— if nobody can see you, nobody can try to shoot at you!

The B-2's long range means it can fly anywhere in the world from its base in Missouri.

All this technology does not come cheap. Each B-2 costs a staggering $2 billion!

SUPER STATS

NORTHROP GRUMMAN B-2 SPIRIT
LENGTH: 69 ft. (20.9 m)
WINGSPAN: 171 ft. (52.12 m)
RANGE: (without refueling) 6,000 miles (9,600 km)
NUMBER OF CREW: 2
NUMBER OF PASSENGERS: 0
TOP SPEED: top secret

LOCKHEED SR-71 BLACKBIRD

Countries across the globe use spy planes to keep an eye on what their enemies are up to. One of the most successful spy planes ever was the SR-71, nicknamed "Blackbird." The idea behind the Blackbird was simple—it would travel really high and really quickly.

Blackbird flew from New York to London in just under 1 hour, 55 minutes. Modern-day passenger jets take around seven hours!

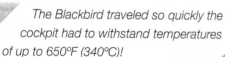

The Blackbird traveled so quickly the cockpit had to withstand temperatures of up to 650°F (340°C)!

Blackbird could travel higher and faster than enemy missiles so it couldn't be shot down!

Blackbird was used by the United States Air Force. It entered service in 1966 and was officially retired in 1998. Blackbird set many flying records. It is still the plane that could fly the highest in level flight. It's also the fastest standard jet plane.

The Blackbird could fly at altitudes of over 85,000 ft. (25,900 m).

SUPER STATS

LOCKHEED SR-71 BLACKBIRD
LENGTH: 55 ft., 7 in. (16.9 m)
WINGSPAN: 107 ft., 3 in. (32.7 m)
RANGE: 2,900+ miles (4,660+ km)
NUMBER OF CREW: 2
NUMBER OF PASSENGERS: 0
TOP SPEED: 2,193 mph (3,530 km/h)

ANTONOV AN-225 MRIYA

The Antonov AN-225 Mriya is a transport plane—but it's no ordinary cargo carrier. The Mriya, which first flew in 1998, is the biggest plane in the world. It can carry cargo weighing up to 550,000 lbs. (250,000 kg). There's enough space to hold 50 cars, or the fuselage (body) of a Boeing 737 airliner.

The Mriya is so heavy that it has to spread its weight across an amazing 32 wheels.

The Mriya is large enough— not to mention powerful enough— to carry a spacecraft on its back.

Mriya is Ukrainian for "dream." It was designed to give a piggyback to Buran, Russia's version of the Space Shuttle. While Buran was being tested, it hitched a ride on top of the Mriya. Buran was not a success and the project was abandoned. However, Mriya survived, and is still flying today.

The Mriya needs an airstrip 2.2 mi. (3.5 km) long in order to take off when fully loaded.

A massive plane needs a lot of power to get it airborne. That's why Mriya has six engines.

The front of the plane lifts up to reveal the cargo-holding area.

SUPER STATS

ANTONOV AN-225 MRIYA
LENGTH: 275 ft., 6 in. (84 m)
WINGSPAN: 290 ft., (88.4 m)
RANGE: (unloaded) 8,699 miles (14,000 km)
NUMBER OF CREW: 6
NUMBER OF PASSENGERS: 0
TOP SPEED: 528 mph (850 km/h)

AIRBUS A380-800

The world's biggest passenger airliner is the Airbus A380-800. It's one of the most modern planes too, using new materials and greener engines to prove it's a real superplane.

The A380 uses less fuel per passenger than any other airliner—which is good news for the environment.

A big plane needs lots of paint, and the A380 has three coats. The paint alone weighs 1,102 lbs. (500 kg)!

More people fly these days than ever before. Plane passengers made 2.75 billion trips in 2011. Busier airports lead to more flights and more fuel being used and more damage to the environment. The answer to the problem might be having bigger planes that use less fuel— planes like the Airbus A380.

The A380 is the world's only completely double-decker plane.

Airlines can decide on how many seats their A380s have. The numbers range from 525 up to 853! No other plane can carry more passengers.

It has 220 windows.

The A380 has quieter engines than other big airliners.

SUPER STATS

AIRBUS A380-800
LENGTH: 239 ft. (72.72 m)
WINGSPAN: 261 ft. (79.75 m)
RANGE: 9,570 miles (15,400 km)
NUMBER OF CREW: 2 (plus flight attendants)
NUMBER OF PASSENGERS: 853
TOP SPEED: 677 mph (1090 km/h)

GULFSTREAM G650

How do the world's most glamorous celebrities, most powerful politicians, and richest tycoons glide from one place to another in complete luxury? They travel by private jet. One of the most luxurious of private jets is the Gulfstream G650.

The turned-up parts at the end of each wing are called winglets. They are like extensions to the wings.

There are twelve different ways of arranging the seating. If none of those is to your liking, you can get a custom-made layout instead!

Even the air inside the G650 is better than in a large passenger jet. It's kept 100% fresh, unlike the recycled air in big planes.

This superplane is bigger, faster, and quieter than most of its rivals. Now that's the way to travel! However, you need deep pockets to own a private jet. A G650 will cost you from around $57 million!

Two Rolls Royce engines provide the power. They have been designed to make less noise than the engines of most private jets.

The cabin interior is 6 ft., 5 in. (1.95 m) high— that's high enough for people to walk around.

SUPER STATS

GULFSTREAM G650
LENGTH: 99 ft., 9 in. (30.4 m)
WINGSPAN: 93 ft., 8 in. (28.55 m)
RANGE: 8,055 miles (12,964 km)
NUMBER OF CREW: 2 (and 2 flight attendants if required)
NUMBER OF PASSENGERS: 18
TOP SPEED: 704 mph (1,133 km/h)

MEAN MACHINES

DORNIER
CD2 SEASTAR

Aircraft need runways to land on—and the bigger the plane, the longer the runway. However, this is not the case with seaplanes. These are a weird cross between boats and aircraft. They are sometimes called flying boats.

Propellers at the back push the plane through the air. Propellers at the front pull the plane forward.

D-ISEA

The Seastar can land on either land or water.

With its boatlike design, the Seastar is happy to spend all its down time on the water.

The Seastar has two engines, one right behind the other. These are called in-line engines.

Seaplanes have been flown for more than 100 years. Today's seaplanes are often light aircraft that have been converted to land on the water. This is not the case with the Dornier CD2 Seastar. This is the first specially built oceangoing seaplane for over 50 years.

The design of the inside of the Seastar can be changed, so the plane can be used to carry cargo or even work as a flying ambulance.

The Seastar's fuselage (body) is made of materials that won't rust.

The passenger area can be arranged with either 12 or 9 seats, or as a more luxurious six-seater with more leg room.

SUPER STATS

DORNIER CD2 SEASTAR
LENGTH: 41 ft., 7 in. (12. 67 m)
WINGSPAN: 58 ft., 2 in. (17.71 m)
RANGE: 978 miles (1,574.2 km)
NUMBER OF CREW: 2 (though just 1 pilot is required)
NUMBER OF PASSENGERS: 12
TOP SPEED: 207 mph (333 km/h)

EDGLEY OPTICA

Sometimes it can be handy to get a bird's eye view of a situation. For example, you might want to keep an eye on traffic, or search for things on the ground. Normal planes travel too fast to get a good look. However, the Edgley Optica is a very different kind of plane.

The Optica is one of the quietest planes around.

The Optica has three seats, so it can be used as a sightseeing plane for tourist trips.

The Edgley Optica was designed to be good at flying at low speeds. This means it's great for observing what's going on below. As a small propeller-driven plane, the Optica is much cheaper to run than a helicopter.

The cockpit of the plane is in front of the fan to give the passengers a clear view. The pilot and passenger can see 270° around them.

The plane is powered through the air by a ducted fan. This is a short propeller sitting inside a round case.

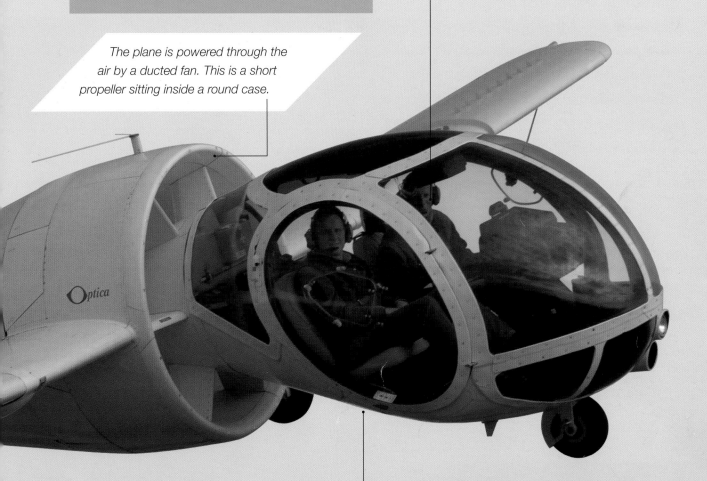

Optica

There's even glass on the floor, so the passengers can see what is below.

SUPER STATS

EDGLEY OPTICA
LENGTH: 26 ft., 6 in. (8.1 m)
WINGSPAN: 39 ft., 4 in. (12 m)
RANGE: 656 miles (1055 km)
NUMBER OF CREW: 1
NUMBER OF PASSENGERS: 2
TOP SPEED: 132 mph (212 km/h)

BOMBARDIER 415

Some superplanes do much more than travel fast or carry heavy loads. These superplanes save lives. The Bombardier 415 is a firefighting seaplane. It is specially designed to tackle forest fires in areas that wheeled vehicles can't get to.

This is the only aircraft designed for aerial firefighting.

A modified version of the 415 is used for air–sea rescues and for observation roles.

The 415 has been designed to land on rough ground as well as on water.

The 415 can scoop up more than 1,600 gallons (6,000 l) of water in one go.

The plane's ability to fly at low speed helps to make sure it drops its load on the right spot.

The trouble with forest fires is that they are usually a long way from the nearest fire hydrant. This means fire crews have nowhere to plug their hoses in. This is where the 415 comes into its own. Once it has dropped its load it can simply fly to the nearest lake or sea and scoop up another load of water before dashing back to the flames.

To scoop up water, the 415 flies along the surface of the lake or sea until its two tanks are full. It is nicknamed the "superscooper."

SUPER STATS

BOMBARDIER 415
LENGTH: 65 ft. (9.8 m)
WINGSPAN: 93 ft., 11 in. (28.6 m)
RANGE: not known
NUMBER OF CREW: 2
NUMBER OF PASSENGERS: 8
TOP SPEED: 207 mph (333 km/h)

PITTS SPECIAL S-2C

Aerobatic displays are incredible spectacles in which planes perform midair stunts. The daredevil pilots fly in tight formations, loop the loop, and narrowly miss each other. These displays draw huge crowds—whether they feature jet planes or superplanes like Pitts Specials.

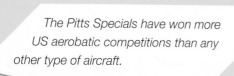

The Pitts Specials have won more US aerobatic competitions than any other type of aircraft.

The Pitts Special is so stable that it can be flown in a straight line without the pilot's needing to touch the hand controls.

Although they look old-fashioned, the Pitts stunt planes are in fact very modern. Like the earliest planes, they have two sets of wings. The extra wings slow the planes down, but give them more lift. And the Pitts Specials use all this lift to perform amazing stunts!

It may be small, but the Pitts Special is incredibly tough. Its rigid body is ideal for twisting and turning through the sky.

The original versions of the Pitts Special had only one seat. Later versions had two, so passengers could enjoy the thrills too.

Spinning the plane around in midair is a popular stunt. The Pitts Special does this very quickly—it can spin 300° every second.

SUPER STATS

PITTS SPECIAL S-2C
LENGTH: 18 ft., 9 in. (5.72 m)
WINGSPAN: 20 ft. (6.1 m)
RANGE: 284 miles (457 km)
NUMBER OF CREW: 1
NUMBER OF PASSENGERS: 1
TOP SPEED: 194 mph (313 km/h)

ZIVKO EDGE 540

Aerobatic displays are really exciting. But what if you want even more skills and thrills? Then perhaps you should check out air racing. This mixes aerobatic ability with a race around a course! The Zivko Edge 540 has won more championships than any other type of racing plane.

Plane wings have flaps called ailerons. These help the plane to steer. The Edge has long flaps for extra maneuvrability.

During the race, the planes have to fly through inflatable 65 ft. (20 m) pylons called "air gates."

The planes are fitted with cameras, which broadcast live during the races.

The Red Bull Air Race series ran from 2003 to 2010. The series staged races right across the globe. The races featured planes trying to navigate their way round a 3–4 mile (5–6 km) course in the fastest time possible. The Zivko Edge 540 was the most successful type of plane to compete.

The race planes leave smoke trails. These are made by injecting fuel onto the exhaust pipes.

The Edge has a very strong body to cope with the pressures of the twisting and turning during a race.

SUPER STATS

ZIVKO EDGE 540
LENGTH: 20 ft., 8 in. (6.3 m)
WINGSPAN: 24 ft., 5 in. (7.43 m)
RANGE: Not known
NUMBER OF CREW: 1
NUMBER OF PASSENGERS: 0
TOP SPEED: 265 mph (426 km/h)

LOCKHEED MARTIN
F-22 RAPTOR

For some pilots, flying a superplane can be a matter of life and death—quite literally. Air force pilots take control of warplanes designed for aerial combat. It's a dangerous job, and not for the faint-hearted. The F-22 Raptor is a warplane flown by the United States Air Force.

The body and frame of the F-22 is made with titanium, which is a very light, but very strong metal.

The F-22 carries missiles for attacking other planes or targets on the ground.

The plane can cruise at speeds of around Mach 1.5. This means it can travel quickly without using a lot of fuel.

Two companies, Lockheed Martin and Boeing, made the F-22 together. It is a fighter plane, built to attack other aircraft or targets on the ground. It is unbelievably quick and highly maneuvrable. Twisting and turning through the air at high speed puts a lot of strain on its tough frame.

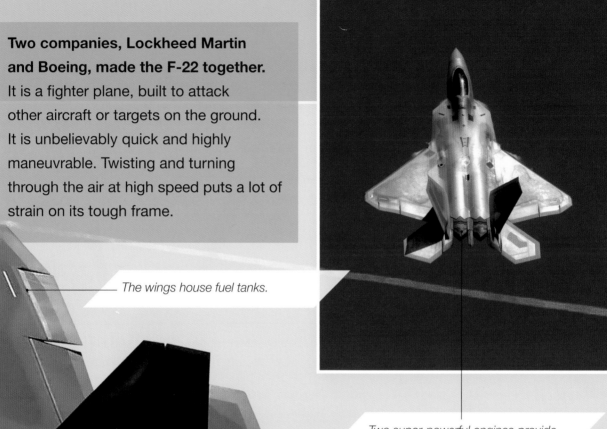

The wings house fuel tanks.

Two super-powerful engines provide more thrust than its rivals.

The F-22 is designed to be difficult to spot on radar.

SUPER STATS

LOCKHEED MARTIN F-22 RAPTOR
LENGTH: 62 ft. (18.9 m)
WINGSPAN: 44 ft., 6 in. (13.56 m)
RANGE: (estimated) 1,860 miles (3,000 km)
NUMBER OF CREW: 1
NUMBER OF PASSENGERS: 0
TOP SPEED: 1,520 mph (2,450 km/h)

VIRGIN GALACTIC SPACESHIP TWO

SpaceShip Two does something really remarkable—it flies so high that it reaches the edge of space itself. At this distance from the Earth, gravity is not as strong. Passengers are able to float around inside!

SpaceShip Two is carried high into the sky by another plane called WhiteKnight Two. This helps to save rocket fuel.

At 50,000 ft. (15,240 m) SpaceShip Two uses its rocket engines to blast off to the edge of space.

The most exciting thing about SpaceShip Two is its passengers. Until now, the only people to have traveled so high above the Earth have been highly trained astronauts. SpaceShip Two gives ordinary people the opportunity to fly right to the edge of space!

You might have to win the lottery before you can travel on SpaceShip Two. It costs around $200,000 for a flight!

The planes take off from a special airport called Spaceport America, in New Mexico.

SUPER STATS

VIRGIN GALACTIC SPACESHIP TWO
LENGTH: 60 ft. (18.28 m)
WINGSPAN: 26 ft., 10 in. (8.2 m)
RANGE: Not available
NUMBER OF CREW: 2
NUMBER OF PASSENGERS: 6
TOP SPEED: 2,284 mph (3,675 km/h)

MEAN MACHINES

GLOSSARY

ailerons a hinged part of a plane's wing that is used to control its movement

airliner a large aircraft that carries passengers

airstrip a piece of land where planes take off and land

altitude height above the sea

booster unit a rocket that carries a craft upward before detaching from it

custom-made built specially for a specific customer

fuselage the body of an aircraft

hydrogen a colorless gas that is found in the air

level not moving up or down

Mach a measurement of speed. Mach 1 is the speed at which sound travels.

maneuvrability ability to move quickly, smoothly and accurately

propeller a machine with spinning blades that pushes a boat or aircraft forward

radar a high-tech system that sends out waves of energy, and uses them to detect aircraft or other vehicles and objects

range the distance that a plane can travel without landing

FURTHER READING

Gilpin, Daniel. *Modern Military Aircraft (Machines Close-Up)*. Benchmark Books, 2010.

Graham, Ian. *Aircraft (Amazing Machines)*. Franklin Watts, 2007.

Kirk, Ellen. *My Plane Book*. Collins, 2006.

Millard, Anne. *DK Big Book of Airplanes*. DK Children, 2001.

Zuehlke, Jeffrey. *Fighter Planes*. First Avenue Editions, 2005.

INDEX